INSPIRATIONAL LIVES

MALALA YOUSAFZAI

EDUCATION CAMPAIGNER

D1073221

Claudia Martin

WAYLAND

First published in 2016 by Wayland
Copyright © Wayland 2016

Wayland, an imprint of
Hachette Children's Group
Part of Hodder & Stoughton
Carmelite House
50 Victoria Embankment
London EC4Y 0DZ

10 9 8 7 6 5 4

 Produced for Wayland by
White-Thomson Publishing Ltd
www.wtpub.co.uk
+44 (0)843 208 7460

Editor: Claudia Martin
Design: Tim Mayer (Mayer Media)
Proofreader and indexer: Izzi Howell

A catalogue record for this title is
available from the British Library.

ISBN: 978 0 7502 9314 3
Library ebook ISBN: 978 0 7502 9011 1
Dewey Number: 323'.092-dc23

Printed in China

An Hachette UK company
www.hachette.co.uk
www.hachettechildrens.co.uk

Picture acknowledgements:
The author and publisher would like
to thank the following for allowing
their pictures to be reproduced in
this publication.
**Alamy/EPA European Pressphoto Agency
b.v.:** front cover, 27; **Al Jazeera English:**
18, 19; **Corbis:** (Muhammad Hamed/
Reuters) 4, (STR/Pakistan/Reuters) 16,
(Stringer/Reuters) 17, (Chris Helgren/
Reuters) 24; **Dreamstime:** (Nuralya) 6,
(Hassan Mohiudin) 7, (Imran Ahmed) 21;
DVIDSHUB: 10; **Vicki Francis/Department
for International Development UK:** 26;
Getty: (Arif Ali/AFP) 5, (Andrew Burton)
8, (Aamir Qureshi/AFP) 11, (Véronique de
Viguerie) 12, 15, 20, (STR/AFP) 14, (Rashid
Mahmood/AFP) 22, (Mohammad Rehman/
AFP) 23, (Queen Elizabeth Hospital
Birmingham) 25; **Shutterstock:** (J Stone)
9, (Map Resources) 13; **Pete Souza/White
House:** 29; **Claude Truong-Ngoc:** 28.

Contents

'Who is Malala?' 4

The birth of a girl 6

Selling books for sweets 8

Kites and classrooms 10

A great earthquake 12

Radio Mullah 14

A day in the life 16

Escape from Mingora 18

Death threats 20

The shooting 22

'Father' and 'country' 24

Back to school 26

'I am Malala' 28

Have you got what it takes
to be an activist? 30

Glossary 31

Index 32

'Who is Malala?'

On 9 October 2012, 15-year-old Malala Yousafzai was travelling home on her school bus in Mingora, Pakistan. She was sitting between her best friend, Moniba, and a girl called Shazia. Suddenly, a bearded young man stepped into the road, bringing them to a halt. A second man leaned in through the window. 'Who is Malala?' he asked.

None of Malala's schoolmates answered, but some of them looked at her. The man pulled out a Colt 45 pistol and fired three bullets at Malala. The first passed through the left side of her head and stuck in her shoulder. Malala slumped into Moniba's lap. The second bullet hit Shazia in the hand. The third travelled through Shazia's shoulder and into her friend Kainat's arm. The bus driver sped off, carrying an **unconscious** Malala and her desperate friends to hospital.

FAST FACT

Malala was named after a famous girl called Malalai of Maiwand (c.1861–80). Malalai led Afghan soldiers to victory against the British in the Battle of Maiwand. She died on the battlefield, aged about 19.

This photo of Malala was taken in 2014 while she was visiting a refugee camp for people who had fled from the war in Syria.

The gunmen were members of an **Islamic** movement called the **Taliban**. Where they took power, the Taliban made people obey their strict **interpretations** of Islamic law. One thing they did was **ban** the education of women. Since 2007, the Taliban had battled the Pakistani government for control of Malala's region: the Swat Valley in Pakistan.

In 2009, when Malala was 11, she wrote a **blog** about trying to continue her education under the threat of the Taliban. Later that year, she started to appear on Pakistani television, standing up for the right of girls to be educated. The Taliban threatened to kill her – but she didn't stop.

As Malala lay in hospital, people took to the streets of Lahore, Pakistan, to protest against the attack.

INSPIRATION

Malala's greatest inspiration is her father, Ziauddin. He ran a chain of boys' and girls' schools and spoke out publicly against the Taliban. He also received **death threats** from them.

The birth of a girl

In a two-room shack in Mingora, a baby girl was born at dawn on 12 July 1997. Mingora is in a mountainous region called the Swat Valley, in northern Pakistan (see the map on page 13). The baby was called Malala.

Mingora is the largest city in the Swat Valley. These women are wearing burqas (loose outer garments).

Malala's father, Ziauddin, could not pay for a hospital birth, so a neighbour helped his wife, Tor Pekai, have her baby. Ziauddin waited anxiously over the road, in the primary school he owned. When Tor Pekai gave birth to a healthy girl, she was filled with happiness – but she was also worried. In Swat, a boy's birth was joyful and marked by the firing of rifles, but a girl's birth was a disappointment. How would Ziauddin react?

Tor Pekai need not have worried. 'When I saw her for the first time, a very newborn child, and I looked into her eyes, I fell in love with her, believe me,' remembers Ziauddin. It was **traditional** to hold a celebration called a Woma (meaning 'seventh') on the seventh day of a baby's life, but Ziauddin could not afford a party. He asked his father for help, but Rohul Amin refused because Malala was a girl.

Ziauddin and Tor Pekai are **Pashtuns**, a people that takes pride in its warrior history. More than 40 million Pashtuns live in northwest Pakistan and neighbouring Afghanistan. Malala's family are members of the Yousafzai tribe, which they use as a surname. They speak Pashto, the Pashtun language, as well as Urdu, the main language of Pakistan. Like nearly everyone in Pakistan and Afghanistan, Pashtuns are Muslims. Muslims believe there is no God but Allah. The holy book of **Islam** is the **Quran**, which Muslims believe contains the words of God, as revealed to the Prophet Muhammad, Peace Be Upon Him.

INSPIRATION

Ziauddin named his school Khushal School, after the Pashtun poet and warrior Khushal Khan Khattak (1613–89). Khattak fought for Pashtun independence using both his sword and the power of his words.

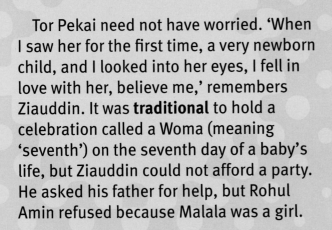

This man is performing a Pashtun dance that was traditionally done by warriors from the Khattak tribe. He is spinning round while holding a sword in either hand.

Selling books for sweets

Ziauddin was born in a **remote** mountain village called Barkana, where none of the houses had electricity. His father, Rohul Amin, was a teacher as well as an **imam** at the local mosque. Rohul Amin was a stern man, but he gave Ziauddin a great belief in the importance of education.

*This is a rare photo of Tor Pekai showing her face in public. She believes she should cover her face with a headscarf as a sign of **modesty**.*

INSPIRATION

Tor Pekai has a deep belief in Islam. The Quran teaches the importance of charity. Tor Pekai always welcomed family, friends and strangers into her home for food and shelter.

Tor Pekai grew up in a village close to Barkana. Ziauddin liked her green eyes and he sent her poems, which she could not read. Tor Pekai had started school when she was six, but had found herself the only girl in a class of boys. She could not see the point in learning to read when girls in Swat were just expected to get married and stay at home. She left before the end of term. Tor Pekai sold her schoolbooks and used the money to buy sweets.

FAST FACT

When Tor Pekai was growing up, only 30% of Pakistani men and 11% of women could read and write. Today, 79% of men and 55% of women are literate.

In 1979, when Ziauddin was 10, the Soviet Union invaded Afghanistan. In the Swat Valley, people were horrified that their fellow Muslims and Pashtuns were under attack. Some men went to Afghanistan to fight. In 1996, a group of Pashtun men battled their way to power in Afghanistan. The group called themselves the Taliban (meaning 'students' in Pashto). Many people in Swat felt the Taliban's beliefs were too extreme, but others were pleased about what was happening in neighbouring Afghanistan.

In the Swat Valley, many husbands and wives are chosen for each other by their families, in arranged marriages. Tor Pekai and Ziauddin were unusual: in 1994, they married because they were in love. Tor Pekai's beliefs and traditions meant she would not take a job outside the home. But when Ziauddin opened the Khushal School, she helped him paint the classroom walls.

Ziauddin believes that everyone – boys and girls, rich and poor – has an equal right to education.

Kites and classrooms

When Malala was a toddler, she liked to wander into lessons at Khushal School. She often sat on a teacher's lap, watching the boys and girls in wonder.

When Malala was two, her parents had a baby boy, whom they named Khushal. Tor Pekai was delighted to have a son. Malala felt her mother favoured Khushal and she sometimes picked fights with him. Five years later, Malala's baby brother Atal was born.

Soon after she turned four, Malala heard the grown-ups talking about something terrible. On 11 September 2001, **terrorists** from a group called **Al-Qaeda** hijacked aeroplanes and flew them into buildings in the United States, killing almost 3,000 people.

US soldiers in Afghanistan. In 2001, soldiers from countries including the USA, UK and Afghanistan removed the Afghan Taliban from power.

Al-Qaeda was linked to the Taliban, so the USA and its **allies** invaded Afghanistan and toppled the Taliban from power. Using aeroplanes called **drones**, the USA also fired missiles at places in Pakistan where the Taliban were hiding. Sometimes they killed ordinary people by accident. Many people in Swat were angry and felt drawn to the Taliban.

When Malala came second to Moniba in a speech-making competition, she realized she had made the mistake of speaking from her notes rather than from her heart.

These pupils are leaving the gate of Khushal School. They are wearing the uniform of white and blue shalwar kameez (tunic and trousers).

When Malala started school, she worked hard to be top of the class. Although it was difficult for girls to have careers, her father encouraged her to aim high. 'Carry on with your dreams,' he told her. Malala's best friend was a kind but bossy girl called Moniba.

As Khushal School started to do well, the family moved into a larger, concrete house with running water and a TV. Malala, her brothers and friends flew kites and played cricket on the house's flat roof. At mealtimes, the family sat on the floor and shared spicy meats, rice and tea.

FAST FACT

All the girls in Malala's class said they wanted to be doctors. They knew their best chance of having a career was as a doctor, which was such a respected job it might be allowed.

A great earthquake

As Malala grew older, she started to worry about what was happening in her part of the world. Life was getting more difficult than ever for girls and women in the Swat Valley. What would her role in life be?

A group called Tehreek-e-Nafaz-e-Shariat-e-Mohammadi (TNSM; 'Movement for the Enforcement of Islamic Law') was gaining power in the valley. They were linked with the Taliban.

More people were turning to the Taliban's strict interpretations of the Quran. They were saying it was wrong for girls to go to school and that women should not leave the home unless they were with a male relative. Many people in Swat had always held these beliefs, but it was getting harder to ignore them.

Even though Malala was a deep thinker, she could be cheeky. She made her friends laugh with jokes and impressions.

INSPIRATION

Khan Abdul Ghaffar Khan (1890–1988) was a Pashtun who **campaigned** against British rule of the region. Malala was struck by the fact that he used only peaceful methods.

The earthquake of October 2005 was centred on northern Pakistan.

In 2003, Malala's father opened a second school: a high school. A year later, he had to split the high school in two, because people told him that if he insisted on teaching girls, he should at least teach them separately from boys. Ziauddin felt the valley was moving backwards. He started to give speeches and send out leaflets about the right of girls to go to school. Malala wrote a letter to Allah. It said: 'God, give me strength and courage and make me perfect because I want to make the world perfect. Malala.'

On the morning of Saturday 8 October 2005, Malala was at school as usual. The ground started to shake. The children shouted, 'Earthquake!' and ran outside in case the building collapsed. Luckily, none of the children was hurt, but across the region 75,000 people were killed. In the next few weeks, it was groups like TNSM who managed to get to Swat's remote villages to give help. This made them even more popular.

FAST FACT

Malala was a big fan of the *Twilight* books by American author Stephanie Meyer. They are about a teenage girl who falls in love with a vampire.

Radio Mullah

The leader of TNSM was called Maulana Fazlullah. In 2007, hundreds of his men moved into the Swat Valley. Fazlullah started preaching on the radio, giving his ideas of good and bad behaviour. TNSM joined forces with the Pakistani Taliban and Fazlullah became leader of the Taliban in the Swat Valley.

Fazlullah spoke on the radio every night. Soon people were calling him Radio Mullah. 'Mullah' means someone educated in Islamic law. He told everyone to stop listening to music, dancing, playing board games and watching TV. He told girls they should not go to school. The Taliban patrolled the streets with guns and punished people who broke their laws.

Maulana Fazlullah led the Taliban in the Swat Valley. The Taliban believe men should have beards, so Fazlullah banned barbers from giving shaves.

FAST FACT

Although the Taliban told girls not to go to school, Malala went every day. She wore ordinary clothes rather than her uniform and hid her books in a shawl on the way there. She was afraid she would be attacked if the Taliban saw her.

At first, many people welcomed the Taliban. Some people burnt their TVs and DVDs in the streets. Other people, including Malala's father, felt the Taliban were wrongly explaining the Quran. Ziauddin believed the Quran values education for everyone, not just boys, and that it does not forbid women to have jobs. Malala, who studied the Quran closely, agreed with him.

TOP TIP

Malala believes that everyone must speak out if they see injustice: 'If people were silent, nothing would change.'

In October 2007, the Pakistani government sent 5,000 soldiers into the Swat Valley and drove the Taliban out. But the Taliban soon came back – and things were worse than before. People who spoke out against the Taliban were murdered. Their bodies were often displayed in Mingora's main square. Bravely, Ziauddin carried on giving his opinion on TV and radio shows.

In September 2008, when she was 11, Malala joined the campaign. Her father took her to the city of Peshawar, where she made a speech to **journalists**: 'How dare the Taliban take away my basic right to education?' she asked.

To spread awareness of the campaign, Malala was photographed in her school uniform by the French photographer Véronique de Viguerie.

A day in the life

In January 2009, the Taliban banned girls' schools in the Swat Valley. The last day that Malala's school was allowed to open was 14 January. On that day, Malala was writing a blog and being filmed for a **documentary**.

A journalist had asked Malala's father for a schoolgirl to write a blog about trying to continue her education under the Taliban. Malala wrote her first blog for the BBC Urdu website on 3 January. The family had also agreed to take part in a documentary for the American *New York Times* website, called *Class Dismissed: Malala's Story*.

FAST FACT

Starting in 2007, the Taliban bombed or burned down more than 400 girls' schools in Swat. They usually waited until everyone had gone home. However, a bomb at the Haji Baba High School killed or injured 10 members of Moniba's family.

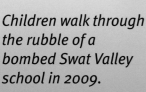

Children walk through the rubble of a bombed Swat Valley school in 2009.

The film crew followed Malala as she went about her last day at school. She had now moved to her father's all-girls high school. Out of the 27 girls who should have been in her class on 14 January, only 11 remained. Fearing for their safety, their parents were either keeping them at home or had sent them to schools outside the Swat Valley.

By writing her blog, Malala hoped to let the world know what the Taliban were doing in Swat.

The girls busied themselves with their lessons until the end of the school day, at 1 pm. But then none of them could bring themselves to leave. Malala wrote in her blog: 'Since today was the last day of our school, we decided to play in the playground a bit longer.' Feeling upset and stressed, Malala and Moniba had a huge row about nothing. When she got home, Malala lay on her bed and cried for hours.

INSPIRATION

It was too dangerous for Malala to write her blog under her real name. She wrote under the pen name Gul Makai. Gul Makai was the heroine of a Pashtun folk tale who used the Quran to teach her elders that war is wrong.

Escape from Mingora

In February 2009, the Taliban agreed to allow girls back to school, as long as they veiled their faces in the street. But most of Malala's classmates had left the Swat Valley. People were afraid, even those who had once supported the Taliban.

Every day, there was news of someone else murdered or beaten. Malala's mother was threatened by the Taliban for going shopping wearing a headscarf rather than a *burqa*. A *burqa* is a long cloak with a veil covering the face. Tor Pekai warned Malala to start covering her face with her headscarf in public.

In May 2009, the Pakistani army sent up to 45,000 soldiers to take back Swat from the Taliban. The army warned everyone to leave the valley for their own safety. On 5 May, Malala and her family, along with friends and cousins, crowded into two cars.

FAST FACT

Malala was horrified by a video she saw on her father's phone. It showed a teenage girl being beaten by the Taliban for leaving the house with a man who was not a relative.

A Pakistani soldier watches the Swat Valley for Taliban movements, on 22 May 2009.

Around 2,200,000 people left the Swat Valley while the army and Taliban battled for control. Many of them found shelter in government camps.

TOP TIP

On 12 July, everyone was too distracted to remember Malala's 12th birthday. Malala felt upset, but she was learning how to put her feelings to one side when there were bigger issues.

Malala packed her precious schoolbooks into a bag, but there was no room for it in the car. Khushal and Atal wanted to bring their pet chickens, but their mother said they would make a mess. Atal suggested buying them nappies, but the chickens stayed behind. Everyone cried, except for Tor Pekai, who knew it was her job to stay calm.

Over the next two months, the army pushed the Taliban out of Swat, killing many of them. They wounded Maulana Fazlullah – but did not catch him. On 24 July, Malala's family returned to Mingora. They saw the rubble of blown-up buildings. At the house, they found their chickens had died. Malala cried with relief when she saw her schoolbooks were safe.

Death threats

There were no walls to keep the Taliban out of the Swat Valley. There was no way to stop men wanting to join them. It was soon clear the Taliban were hiding everywhere. People who spoke against them were often killed.

Malala, her father and their friends continued to campaign against the Taliban. Malala often appeared on Pakistani TV. She argued not only for girls' education but also for the rights of street children, who usually did not go to school.

Malala's work started to be noticed around the world. She was given awards. Tor Pekai was worried that Malala's fame would draw the Taliban's attention to her. Malala's father had received more than one death threat from the Taliban.

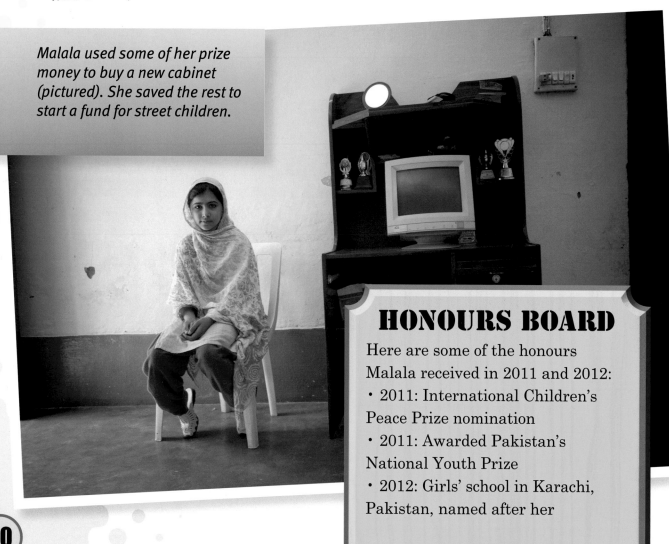

Malala used some of her prize money to buy a new cabinet (pictured). She saved the rest to start a fund for street children.

HONOURS BOARD

Here are some of the honours Malala received in 2011 and 2012:
- 2011: International Children's Peace Prize nomination
- 2011: Awarded Pakistan's National Youth Prize
- 2012: Girls' school in Karachi, Pakistan, named after her

INSPIRATION

When her campaign took her to Pakistan's large cities, Malala met women who were journalists, politicians, doctors and lawyers. She saw how different life could be just a few hundred kilometres away.

These men are Taliban members who have been captured by the Pakistani army. The man in front is talking about different ways of understanding Islamic law.

In January 2012, Malala was told the Taliban had posted a threat to kill her on the Internet. Her response was brave: 'Even if they come to kill me, I will tell them what they are trying to do is wrong, that education is our basic right.' The Taliban had never killed a girl, so Malala thought it was her father who was really at risk. She refused to be sent away to boarding school. But despite her courage, Malala was afraid.

At night, Malala checked that every gate, door and window in the house was locked. She said all five of her daily prayers. Usually, she missed out the afternoon prayer when she was watching TV. Her mother insisted that she stop walking to and from school. From now on, she would take a rickshaw to school and ride home on the school bus.

The shooting

On the day she was shot, Malala arrived in school an hour later than usual, at 9 am, because it was exam time. She spent the morning taking a tricky Pakistan studies test. By midday, Malala was waiting for the school bus to take her home. She chatted with Moniba as she ate a corn cob.

When the bus was ready, all the other girls covered their faces with their headscarves as they ran into the street. Malala, as usual, chose to leave her face uncovered. The bus driver showed them a magic trick with a pebble as Malala, Moniba, Kainat, Shazia, 16 other girls and three teachers packed onboard.

The police examine Malala's school bus for evidence.

It was as the bus passed the snack factory that the two gunmen stepped into the street. Malala did not get a chance to speak as one of them leaned in through the back of the bus and shot her, also hitting Kainat and Shazia. At the same time, Tor Pekai was beginning her first lesson with Malala's old nursery teacher. Malala's mother had decided to learn to read.

When Ziauddin got to Swat Central Hospital, he found Malala lying unconscious on a trolley. He was gripped by fear. Malala's headmistress, Madam Maryam, arrived. The doctors told her that a scan had shown the bullet passed through Malala's forehead but missed her brain. At 3 pm, Malala, her father and Maryam were taken by helicopter to a military hospital in Peshawar.

INSPIRATION

Madam Maryam showed Malala what a determined woman could achieve in the Swat Valley. She was a respected teacher who often risked her safety to help her pupils.

Someone rushed to tell Tor Pekai, but in the panic no one thought to drive her to hospital. She could not go alone. As she heard the helicopter fly over her house, she ran on to the roof – she knew her beloved daughter was onboard.

Malala on a hospital stretcher shortly after the shooting. Kainat and Shazia were also treated in hospital and made full recoveries.

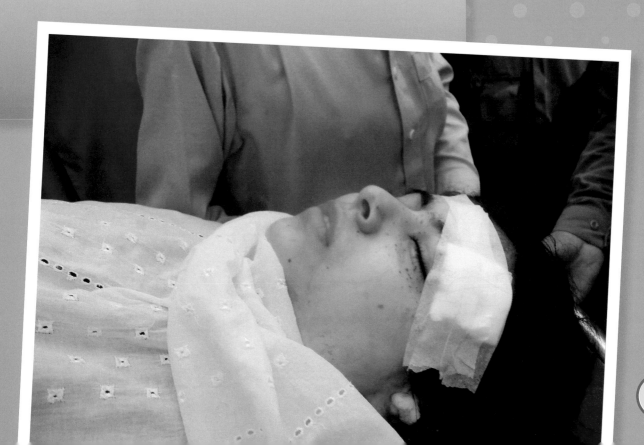

'Father' and 'country'

At 1.30 am, Malala's doctors operated on her. A piece of bone had entered her brain, making it swell. The doctors needed to take out a portion of skull to give her brain more room. They also had to remove the bullet from her shoulder.

Malala's mother and Atal had reached the hospital during the evening. As her family prayed, news of the attack was spreading around the world. The operation was a success, but over the next hours and days, Malala got worse rather than better. Ziauddin felt it was all his fault.

On 15 October, Malala was flown to Queen Elizabeth Hospital in Birmingham, England. Everyone felt this was her best chance of making a full recovery. Six days had passed since the shooting. Malala was still unconscious. The Pakistani government gave a passport only to Ziauddin. He felt he could not leave his wife and sons without protection, so they all stayed behind.

An ambulance carries Malala from the aeroplane to the hospital in Birmingham.

INSPIRATION

While Malala was in hospital, she read *The Wizard of Oz* by L. Frank Baum. Malala was inspired by the character Dorothy, who tries to help others as she struggles along the yellow brick road towards her goal.

On 16 October, Malala woke up. She found herself in a shiny hospital room where everyone spoke English but looked as if they came from many different countries. She wanted to know where she was and where her family were, but she could not speak. She wrote two words on a notepad: 'father' and 'country'. When she was given a mirror, she was shocked by her shaved hair and lopsided face. The bullet had damaged a nerve in the left side of her face, making it droop. Malala's family was finally able to join her on 26 October.

FAST FACT

When Malala came round, she realized how famous she had become. People from all over the world had sent toys and flowers. She was very pleased by a message from Hollywood actress Angelina Jolie.

Khushal, Ziauddin and Atal at Malala's bedside in Birmingham. Tor Pekai has kept her back to the camera.

Back to school

In January 2013, Malala was well enough to leave hospital. Although the family desperately wanted to return to Mingora, it was too dangerous. They had to build a new life in Birmingham.

Today the Taliban do not have any bans against girls' education. The Pakistani government is working hard to get all its children into school in the near future.

In November 2012, Malala had had an operation to rebuild the nerve on the left side of her face. This allowed her to smile again, but sometimes her left eyelid still droops when she is talking. In February 2013, another operation put a metal plate in her skull and an **implant** in her left ear so she can hear.

FAST FACT

At the time of writing, Taliban members had been arrested for Malala's shooting, but it was not clear if the gunman had been caught. In November 2013, Maulana Fazlullah rose to become leader of the Pakistani Taliban.

Malala's father was given the job of education **attaché** in Pakistan's Birmingham **consulate**. The family moved to a house in a quiet corner of the city. Malala was delighted to discover that, for a little while, she could treat her brothers however she liked. Tor Pekai felt lonely without her friends and family. Unlike her husband and children, she could not speak English. At first, she was shocked by the revealing clothes that British girls wore even in the terrible English weather.

Malala started at a girls' school in Birmingham in April 2013. She was put in a class with girls two years younger so she had time to study for her GCSEs. This was tough for a girl who had always taken pride in being top of her year. She found it hard to make friends, as everyone saw her as 'the girl who was shot by the Taliban' rather than just Malala. But Malala was not discouraged. She was determined to do well at school, so that she could fight her campaign with even more strength.

Malala walks to school in Birmingham on her first day.

TOP TIP

Malala feels it is wonderful to go to school in Britain without fear. Her advice to British children is to value their education.

'I am Malala'

The Taliban did not keep Malala quiet. Her determination to speak up has only grown. Today, she travels across the world, campaigning for the rights of girls. She also speaks out for all children whose lives are destroyed by **conflict**.

While Malala was in hospital, people took up the **slogan** 'I am Malala'. It was an answer to the Taliban gunman's question: 'Who is Malala?' They meant that we should all stand together to speak for those who cannot speak for themselves. A worldwide education **petition** was started, called 'I am Malala'. It led to the Pakistani government passing a Right to Education Bill, setting out plans to get all Pakistani children into school.

MALALA YOUSAFZAI

In 2013, Malala was awarded the Sakharov Prize by the European Parliament for her defence of human rights. A previous winner was Nelson Mandela.

HONOURS BOARD

• 2013: Voted one of *Time* magazine's 100 Most Influential People

• 2013: International Campaigner of the Year

• 2013: Pride of Britain Award

• 2014: Awarded the Nobel Peace Prize for her work for children

On her 16th birthday, 12 July 2013, Malala gave her first public speech since the shooting. This speech was at the **United Nations** in New York. She said: 'Let us pick up our books and our pens. They are our most powerful weapons.' The day was named Malala Day. The plan is to hold Malala Day every year to remind us of the millions of children not in school.

Malala believes that most of the world's problems could be solved by education – rather than with weapons. She believes that conflict is caused by lack of understanding. She believes that educating more people to be doctors could stop the spread of disease. Malala now leads a charity that works for girls' education, called the Malala Fund.

In October 2014, Malala was called out of her classroom to be told that she had won the Nobel Peace Prize. She is the youngest person ever to be given the world-famous award.

FAST FACT

In 2014, 58 million children across the world aged 6 to 11 were not in school. 31 million of them were girls and 27 million were boys. Many of them lived in areas shaken by conflict.

In October 2013, Malala met the president of the USA, Barack Obama, his wife Michelle and daughter Malia. She was not afraid to ask him to stop US drone strikes in Pakistan.

Have you got what it takes to be an activist?

1) If you saw someone being bullied, would you speak up for them?
a) I always speak up when I see unfairness or unkindness.
b) I stand up for anyone who looks like they need my help.
c) Bullying is horrible and I hope I would do the right thing.

2) Are you interested by what's going on in the world? Do you read young people's newspapers?
a) I take a keen interest in the news and have my own opinions.
b) The news is often a bit too complicated or scary for me.
c) I am really interested in lots of news stories, but I don't know how I could get involved.

3) Do you work hard at school?
a) I always do my best, however difficult the work is.
b) I am never put off by hard work, particularly if I'm interested in the subject.
c) I know I am lucky to be able to go to school, but it's not easy to remember that on a Friday afternoon.

4) Are you good at getting your ideas across to people? Do you like making speeches?
a) I enjoy telling people what I think, even if it's in front of the whole school.
b) If I have something interesting to say, nothing stops me from saying it.
c) I have lots of ideas but sometimes I feel shy about putting up my hand.

5) Do you believe in anything passionately? Would you be prepared to make yourself unpopular by standing up for it?
a) I have strong beliefs and I will always defend them.
b) I would stand up for the right cause, but there's nothing I feel passionately about yet.
c) I feel passionately about my beliefs, but I get nervous if I'm the only person speaking out.

6) Once you have set yourself a goal, do you have the determination to stick to it?
a) I always achieve what I set out to do, even if the road is long and hard.
b) I have plenty of determination. When I find the right goal, I will achieve it.
c) There are lots of things I want to achieve, but it's easy to get distracted or downhearted.

RESULTS

Mostly As: You have got what it takes to be an activist: belief, courage and determination. Always remember to listen to others' views before you decide to fight for a cause.

Mostly Bs: You have the determination and bravery to be an activist. You have not yet found a cause you believe in enough to fight for, so carry on learning about the world.

Mostly Cs: You have strong ideas about what is right and wrong. For now, try lots of different activities so you can build your self-confidence. If you work hard, one day you will make an excellent activist.

Glossary

activist Person who tries to bring about change, using peaceful methods such as protesting or making speeches.

allies Countries that help one another.

Al-Qaeda A network of terrorists that carries out attacks in the name of Islam.

attaché Diplomat (representative of a country abroad) who has responsibility for a particular area.

ban Not allow; make something off-limits.

blog Website or webpage that shows a series of 'posts', or entries, which were written at different times. The posts often contain the writer's personal experiences or opinions.

campaigned Worked towards a goal, using methods such as speeches and leaflets.

conflict War or violent struggle.

consulate Office belonging to one country in another country.

death threats Promises to kill another person, often with the aim of making that person behave in a particular way.

documentary Film or TV programme that presents facts about an event or person.

drones Aircraft that are operated by remote control, without pilots.

hospitable Treating guests generously.

imam Leader of prayers in a mosque.

implant Device placed in the body.

interpretations Explanations of a book or other work. Each person's interpretation may be influenced by their own opinions.

Islam The religion of Muslims. Muslims believe that there is one God and that His prophet is Muhammad, Peace Be Upon Him. Muslims also believe in the importance of charity, prayer, fasting during the month of Ramadan, and making a pilgrimage to Mecca (birthplace of the Prophet) once in their lives.

Islamic Relating to, or in support of, Islam.

journalists People who write about the news or who report it on TV or the radio.

literate Able to read and write.

modesty Goodness, respectfulness and not having too much pride in one's appearance.

Pashtuns A people living mainly in Afghanistan and neighbouring Pakistan.

petition Written request for change that is signed by a large number of people.

Quran The holy book of Islam, originally written in Arabic. It contains guidance on how to live a good life.

remote Far away; hard to reach.

slogan Phrase that expresses the aims or beliefs of a group.

Taliban Extreme Islamic group that grew up among Pashtuns in Afghanistan.

terrorists People who use violence, or the threat of violence, to achieve their goals.

traditional The way things have been done for a long time.

unconscious Unable to respond; unaware of one's surroundings.

United Nations International organization that aims to create peace and progress.

Index

Afghanistan 7, 9, 10, 11
Al-Qaeda 10–11
army, Pakistani vs Taliban 15, 18–19
army, US vs Taliban 10, 11
arranged marriage 9
awards 20, 28

ban on girls' education 5, 16–17, 18
Birmingham, new life in 26–27
birth of Malala 6
blog 5, 16, 17
bombing of schools 16
burqa 6, 18

campaigning, Malala 5, 15, 16–17, 20, 27, 28–29
campaigning, Ziauddin 13, 15, 20

death threats 5, 20–21
documentary 16–17
drones 11, 29

earthquake 13
education, right to 9, 15, 20, 21, 28, 29

fame 24, 25, 28, 29
Fazlullah, Maulana 14, 19, 22, 26

government, Pakistani 5, 15, 24, 26, 28
Gul Makai (pen name) 17

headscarves 8, 18, 22
hospital, Pakistan 23, 24
hospital, UK 24–25
house, Malala's 6, 11, 19, 27

Islam 5, 7, 8, 14

Kainat (friend) 4, 22, 23
Khushal School 7, 9, 10, 11, 13, 16–17, 20

literacy 8, 9, 23

Madam Maryam (headmistress) 23
Malala Day 29
Malala Fund 29
Mingora 4, 6, 15, 19, 26
Moniba (best friend) 4, 11, 16, 17, 22

Obama, Barack 29
operations, medical 24, 26

Pashtuns 6, 7, 9, 12, 17
Peshawar 15, 23

Quran, the 7, 8, 12, 15

school bus 4, 21, 22
school in Pakistan, Malala's time at 11, 14, 16–17, 22
schoolbooks 8, 14, 19
September 11, 2001 10
Shazia (friend) 4, 22, 23
shooting of Malala 4, 22–23

Swat Valley, life in 5, 6, 7, 8, 9, 13, 14
Swat Valley, military operations in 15, 18–19
Swat Valley, response to Taliban in 9, 11, 12, 15, 18

Taliban, attitude to girls' education 5, 12, 14, 16–17, 18, 26
Taliban, beginning of 9
Taliban, beliefs of 5, 9, 12, 14
Taliban, life under 12, 14–15, 16, 18, 20–21
terrorism 10, 16
TNSM (Movement for the Enforcement of Islamic Law) 12, 13, 14

women, life of in Swat Valley 6, 7, 8, 9, 11, 12, 13, 18, 23

Yousafzai, Atal (brother) 10, 11, 19, 24, 25, 27
Yousafzai, Khushal (brother) 10, 11, 19, 25, 27
Yousafzai, Rohul Amin (grandfather) 7, 8
Yousafzai, Tor Pekai (mother) 6, 7, 8–9, 19, 20, 21, 23, 24, 25, 27
Yousafzai, Ziauddin (father) 5, 6, 7, 8–9, 13, 15, 20, 21, 23, 24, 25, 27